AF604601
VOTE
VOTE
VOTE

GOVERNMENT
IN AUSTRALIA
AUSTRALIAN
PARLIAMENT
John Lesley
REDBACK
publishing

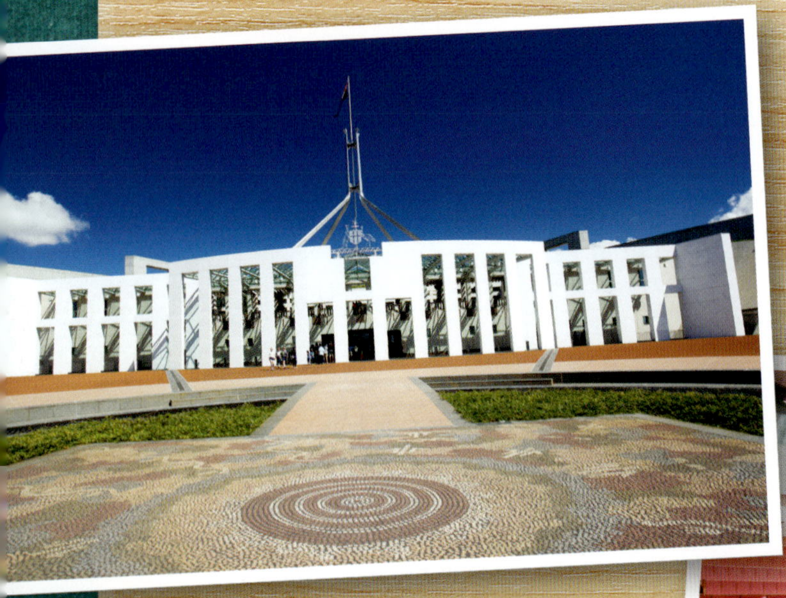

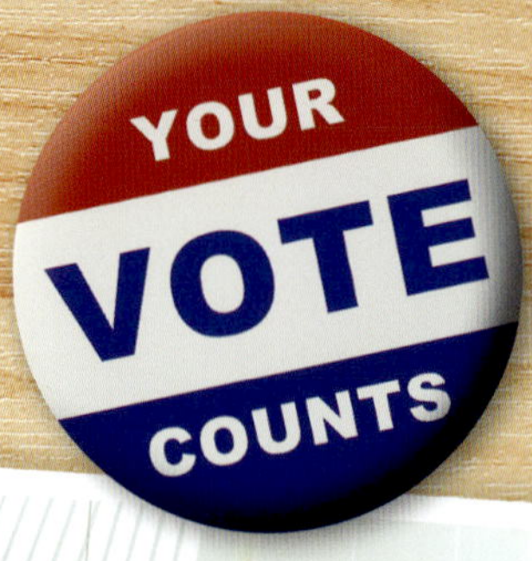

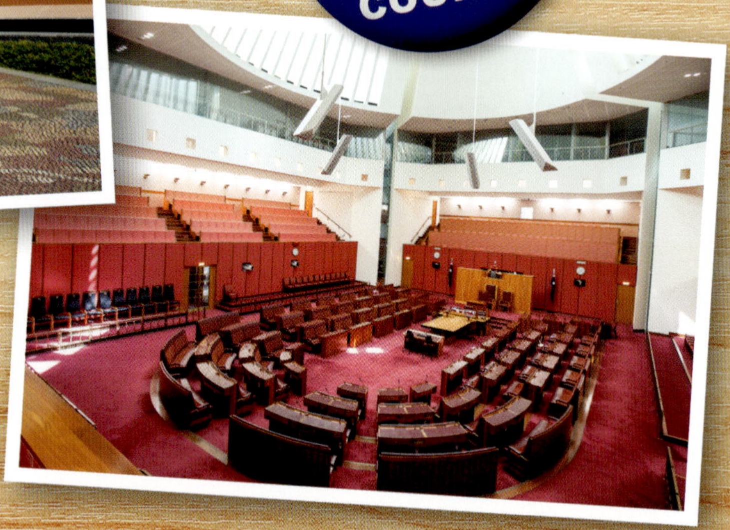

First Published 2025 by
Redback Publishing
Suite 6, 13a Narabang Way,
Belrose NSW 2085
Australia

www.redbackpublishing.com
orders@redbackpublishing.com

ISBN 978-1-761401-09-1

Author: John Lesley
Editor: Caroline Thomas
Designer: Redback Publishing

Original illustrations © Redback Publishing 2025
Originated by Redback Publishing

A catalogue record for this book is available from the National Library of Australia

CONTENTS

AUSTRALIAN PARLIAMENT

What Is It?

Australia's first Prime Minister Edmund Barton (1849-1920)

When we think of the Australian Parliament, most of us have in mind the images we have seen on television of politicians speaking in a large hall with either red or green seating and carpet. There is much more to the whole Parliament than this.

The Australian Parliament is not a place. It is the whole organisation that is responsible for making laws that result in government being carried out. It is sometimes also called the Commonwealth Parliament or the Federal Parliament. Its existence is based on rules in the Constitution, which resulted in the creation of the Commonwealth of Australia in 1901.

The Australian Parliament is located in Parliament House in Canberra. It has been located in other places since its formation in 1901, and it operated as a Parliament even before there was a Parliament House built for it.

The Australian Parliament Has Three Sections:

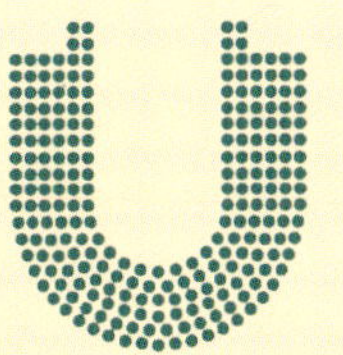

1 The House of Representatives (the Lower House)

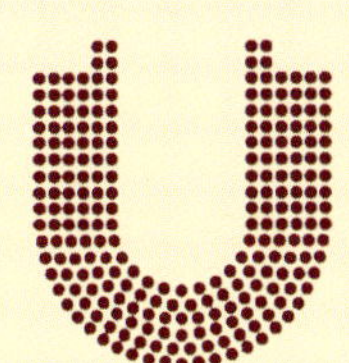

2 The Senate (the Upper House)

3 The Monarch (represented in Australia by the Governor-General)

These three bodies work together to create the laws and therefore the government of Australia.

The Lower House

Bicameral System

Australia has a bicameral system of government, which means that it has two separate Houses of Parliament, with each having a separate role in lawmaking for the Nation.

The Upper House

Australia first parliament opened on 9 May, 1901 in Melbourne

The Australian Parliament includes all the elected representatives, not just those who have formed the Government after an election.

THE HOUSE OF REPRESENTATIVES (Lower House)

Purpose

The House of Representatives, or Lower House, is one of the two Houses of the Australian Parliament. Its MPs introduce, debate and pass Bills that will become laws that Australian citizens live by.

YOUR VOTE COUNTS

Crosschecking votes at the Federal election

MP – "Member of Parliament"

There are 151 Members of Parliament elected to the House of Representatives. They are called MPs and are entitled to use the term MP after their name.

MPs are elected from an electorate in their State and they represent the wishes of the people who elected them. They also represent those who did not vote for them in their electorate, and any voter in that area can speak with their local member or seek their assistance on relevant matters. When they are not sitting in Parliament in Canberra, most MPs go back to their electorate office and work to become familiar with the needs and wishes of their constituents.

The Green House

The furnishings in the House of Representatives are a gumtree-green. The traditional colour for the Lower House in the British Parliament is green, so a local version of this colour was used for the Australian colour scheme as well.

The Lower House of the Australian Parliament

The Lower House of the British Parliament

Government and Opposition

The political party with the majority of MPs elected to the House of Representatives at a Federal election forms the Government. The party with the next largest number of elected Members forms the Opposition. The MPs have a term of three years, after which they have to stand for and win another election if they wish to remain in the House of Representatives. The party numbers in the Senate do not affect which party will form Government.

If an MP dies or leaves Parliament mid-term, there is a by-election for a replacement.

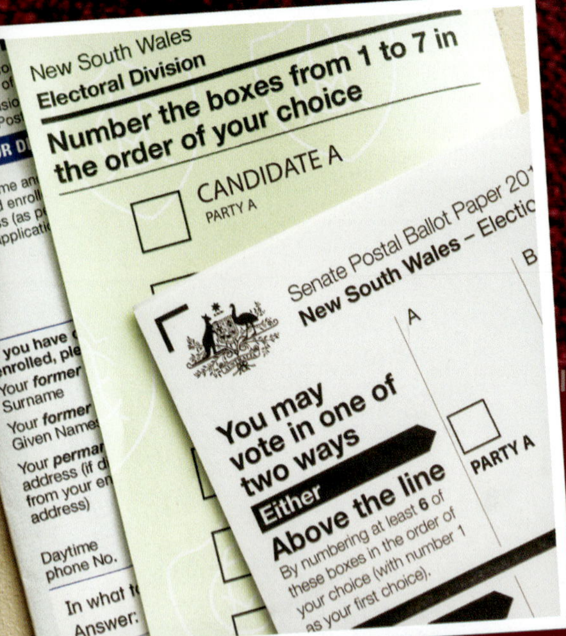

THE SENATE

(Upper House)

The House of Review

The Senate, or Upper House, is one of the two Houses of the Australian Parliament. Its Senators can introduce Bills, but mostly they review Bills that are sent to them by the Lower House. A Bill cannot become a law unless it is voted on and accepted by both Houses of Parliament. This is why the Senate is often called the 'house of review'. Having a house with the authority to reject any Bill is an important aspect of Australian democracy, since it helps to ensure that any proposed legislation is thoroughly scrutinised, and changed if necessary, before it can become a law.

Senate Elections

Senators are elected for the whole State or Territory that they want to represent. There are twelve Senators elected for each State and two each for the Australian Capital Territory and the Northern Territory. There are 76 Senators in the Australian Senate.

Senators are elected for six years, but they are not all elected at the same time. The six States are split into two groups of three, which take turns at holding a Senate election every three years. The Senators from the two Territories,

the Australian Capital Territory and the Northern Territory face election every three years, at the same time as the Members of the House of Representatives.

If a Senator dies or leaves Parliament mid-term, a replacement Senator is chosen by the Parliament of the State for which they were elected.

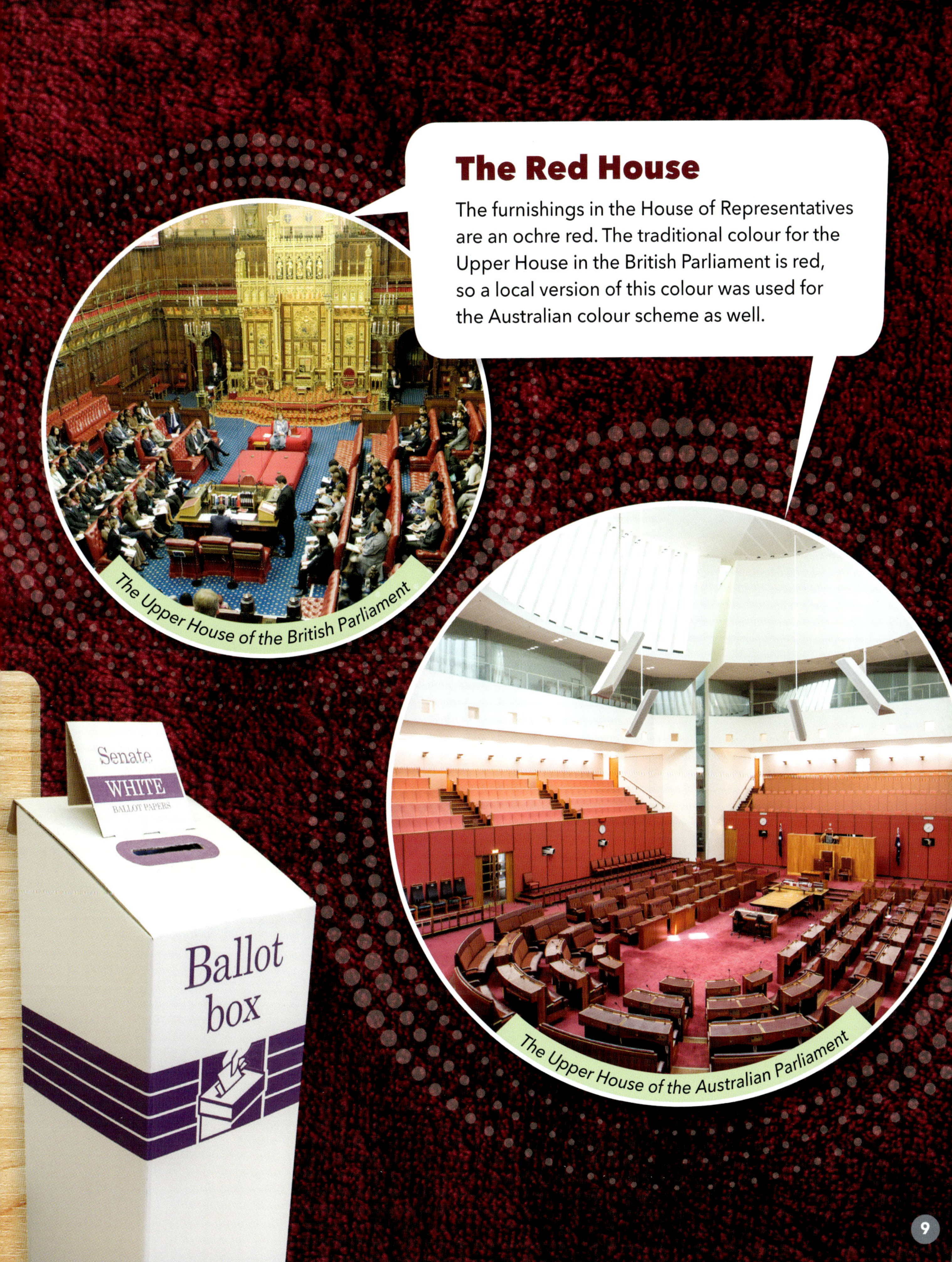

The Red House

The furnishings in the House of Representatives are an ochre red. The traditional colour for the Upper House in the British Parliament is red, so a local version of this colour was used for the Australian colour scheme as well.

MONARCH & GOVERNOR-GENERAL

Head of Parliament

The head of the Australian Parliament is not the Prime Minister or any other elected person. It is the British Monarch, currently King Charles III. Since the Monarch is not in Australia, they are represented by the Governor-General.

Charles III, King of the United Kingdom and the Commonwealth realms

General Sam Mostyn, the 28th Governor-General of Australia

Westminster System

Australia has a Westminster System of government that originated in Britain and was later adopted by former British colonies when they became self-governing. Examples of countries with a Westminster System include Australia, New Zealand and Canada, which all have the British Monarch as their Head of State.

Westminster System Guide

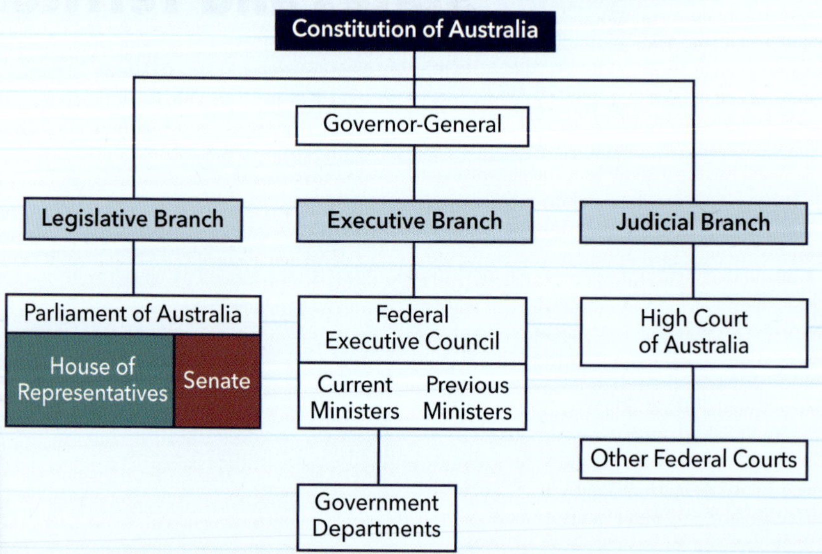

States and Territories

The six States and two Territories of Australia also have Westminster System governments, with a representative of the Monarch as their head. In the States, the representative is called a Governor, who is completely independent of the Australian Governor-General.

The Northern Territory does not have its own independent head. Instead, the Governor-General of Australia appoints an Administrator who performs many of the duties of a governor. The Australian Capital Territory has no head who represents the Monarch.

FORMING A GOVERNMENT

Highest Number Wins

The word 'Government' refers to the group of politicians which has the highest number of elected people in the House of Representatives. In the Westminster System, this group is usually a political party. The party with the next highest number of elected politicians becomes the official Opposition.

Swearing In

Before a Government is formed, the Governor-General, on behalf of the Monarch, swears in the Prime Minister and the Ministers. A Minister is an elected representative appointed by the Prime Minister to head one of the departments of government. A department is a body set up to ensure the policies of the Government are carried out. The daily administration of a department is run by public servants.

King Charles III

Oath of Allegiance

The Australian Constitution states that elected politicians need to swear that they will bear allegiance to the Crown as follows:

"Every senator and every member of the House of Representatives shall before taking his seat make and subscribe before the Governor-General, or some person authorised by him, an oath or affirmation of allegiance"

The elected politician cannot take part in Parliament until they take the oath of allegiance.

PARLIAMENT HOUSE

Old and New Parliament Houses

The Australian Parliament has met in Parliament House in Canberra since 1988. Before then, meetings were held in other locations. Immediately after Federation in 1901, the first Parliament met in the Exhibition Building in Melbourne, and then continued meeting in the Victorian Parliament House building until 1927, when a Parliament House was finally built in Canberra. This building is still standing, but it is no longer used as Parliament House, since the new building replaced it in 1988.

The modern Parliament House building uses symbolic designs and colours, both inside and outside.

What To Wear

There are dress standards for politicians, journalists and special guests in Parliament House:

"standards should involve good trousers, a jacket, collar and tie for men and a similar standard of formality for women"

Open Space

Between the two Houses is an open space where all the elected representatives can gather. This provision comes from the British Parliament in Westminster, where the hallway between the two Houses has been, for hundreds of years, a place where politicians can meet and talk before they enter their own House.

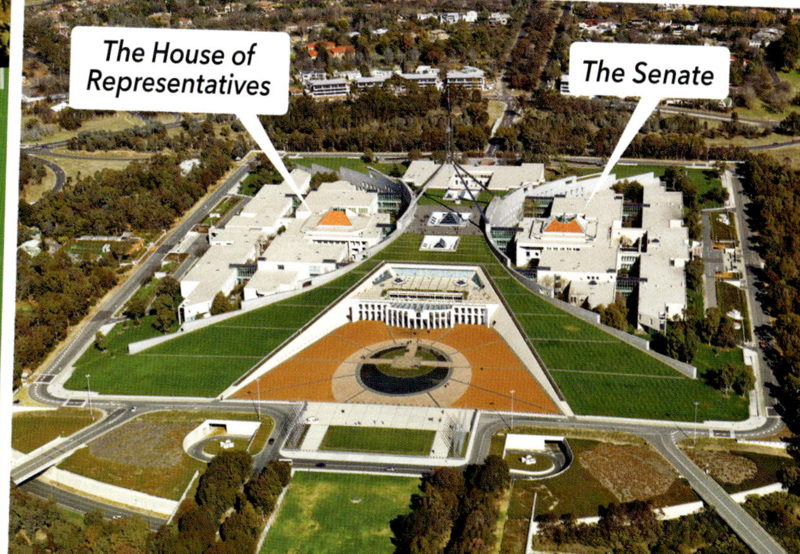

TRADITIONS IN PARLIAMENT

The British Usher of the Black Rod tradition is also used in Australia's Parliament

Usher of the Black Rod

Australia has borrowed many of the traditions and customs of the British Parliament. One of these is the position of Usher of the Black Rod in the Senate.

The Usher always carries the Black Rod when performing official duties, such as knocking on the door of the House of Representatives (the Lower House) to tell them to move to the Senate and attend the opening ceremony of a new Parliament. This custom comes from nearly 400 years ago, when Charles I was King. At that time, the House of Commons closed the door and would not let the King enter. The Black Rod was used to forcefully knock on the door and let the politicians know that the King was not pleased with being locked out!

Senate Only

Even now, the Governor-General, who acts in place of the Monarch, does not enter the Australian House of Representatives. When Queen Elizabeth II visited Australia in the past, she only ever spoke in the Senate, and not in the Lower House.

Dawdling Politicians

If you notice politicians from the Lower House dawdling and chatting while walking to the Senate, when ordered to do so by the Usher of the Black Rod, this is also a tradition. It was the way British politicians from the time of Charles I behaved, to show the King that he did not have all the power in Parliament.

The use of a symbolic mace originates from the British Parliament

The Mace

The Mace is a symbolic, gilded staff carried by the Serjeant-at-arms on ceremonial occasions in the House of Representatives.

The Mace looks like a weapon because that is the origin of its use. It used to be needed for the Sergeant-at-arms to do his work of keeping order and making arrests. Today, the Mace represents the authority of the Speaker of the House of Representatives. The Serjeant-at-arms in the Australian Parliament is still responsible for maintaining order and removing people from the House if necessary. School visits to Parliament are managed by the Serjeant-at-arms.

'Serjeant' or 'Sergeant'?

The unusual spelling of 'serjeant' instead of the modern way 'sergeant' is a result of the historical spelling used for the role by the British Parliament.

Despatch Boxes

Two ornate, silver and wooden boxes sit on tables at the centre of the House of Representatives, in front of the Prime Minister and the Leader of the Opposition.

The boxes remind us of a tradition of using boxes in the British Parliament to hold important documents.

Welcome to Country

Australia has created a new tradition in the form of a Welcome to Country ceremony. These have been held before the opening of a new Parliament since 2008.

IT'S THE LAW

From Bill to Law

Making Laws

When making laws, the Australian Parliament follows the set of rules in the Constitution. This document restricts its law-making powers to matters which include income tax, pensions, postal services, marriage laws, defence, immigration, how Australia interacts with other nations, international trade and a few other subjects. Laws that affect the way schools are run, for example, are not part of the responsibility of the Australian Parliament.

The Australia Parliament makes laws for a range of matters including defence

PASSAGE OF A BILL

Before a Bill becomes law, it goes through the following stages:

Stage 1
A draft of the law is written. This is called a Bill.

Stage 2
The Bill is debated in the House of Representatives and voted on.

Stage 3
If the Bill is passed by the majority of the Members, it goes to the Senate.

Working Together

The House of Representatives, the Senate and the Governor-General work together to govern Australia and make laws. Members of either the House of Representatives or the Senate can introduce Bills, but most Bills are introduced in the House of Representatives.

Stage 4

The Senate votes on the Bill.

Stage 5

If the Bill is passed in the Senate, it goes to the Governor-General for signing.

Stage 6

Once the Governor-General signs the Bill, it becomes an Act of Parliament.

Stage 7

The new law comes into effect at a set date, which may not be the same date that the Governor-General signs the Bill.

What is Royal Assent?

Royal Assent is the term used for the signing of a Bill into law by the Governor-General. It means that the Monarch has approved the new law through their local representative, the Governor-General.

Common Law

There is another type of law in Australia that is not made by politicians voting in Parliament. This is called common law, and it is made by judges in courts. A judge's decision in court may set a 'precedent', so that if the same set of circumstances arises in the future, the original decision may need to be followed as if it were a law.

SEPARATION OF POWERS

The Australian Constitution outlines how the power to make and manage Australian law is given to three independent bodies:

The Judiciary

Comprises the High Court and Federal courts.

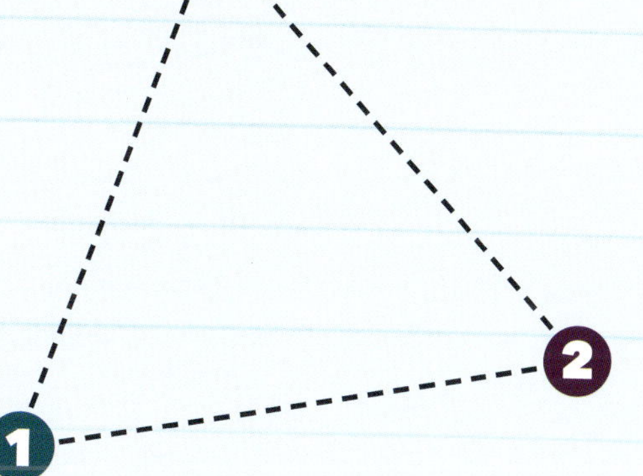

The Australian Parliament

Comprises the Monarch or Governor-General, the Senate and the House of Representatives.

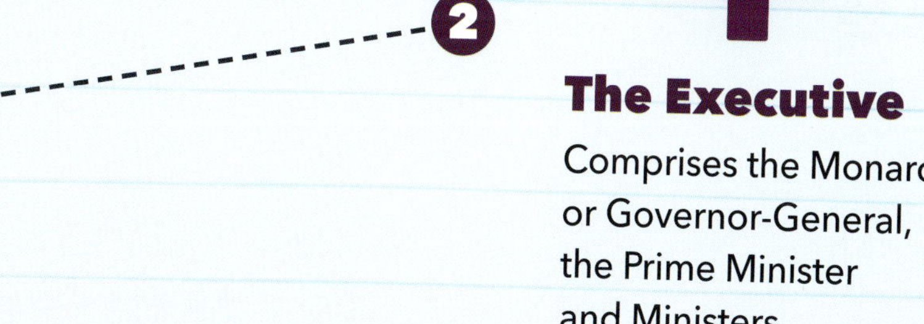

The Executive

Comprises the Monarch or Governor-General, the Prime Minister and Ministers.

Reducing Risk

This division is based on the principle of the 'separation of powers', which reduces the risk of any one of the three parts of government gaining absolute power.

HIGH COURT

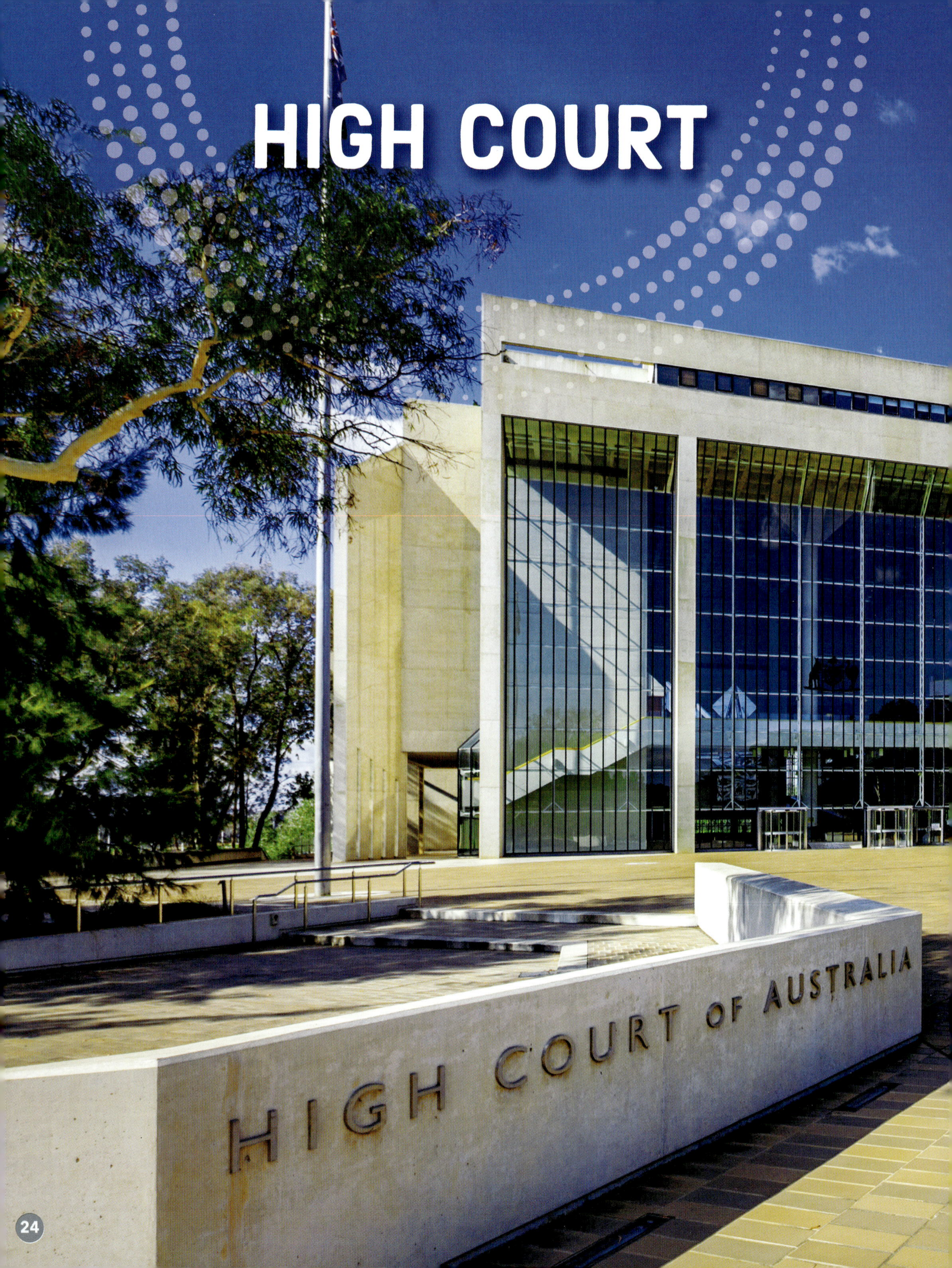

A court is a body headed by a judge or magistrate. Its role is to interpret laws and make decisions on penalties to be applied to any person or organisation that does not follow the law.

The High Court of Australia is located in Canberra

Origins

The High Court is the highest court in Australia. It was established in 1901 as a vital part of the new Parliament. It is headed by seven Justices who together make decisions on matters brought before them.

Appeal Process

People who are unhappy with a decision made in certain other courts across Australia may make an appeal to the High Court to review the decision.

COMMITTEES

Committees are a way that ordinary people can have a say on Bills or on other major aspects of life in Australia that are being discussed in Parliament.

Speeding Up the System

Before politicians vote on Bills or make them into law, they may form a Committee to discuss the details. This Committee meets outside the House and goes through all the details of concern. In this way, the Committee stops the whole parliamentary system being slowed down by discussions on just one Bill.

Write or Attend

People who wish to have their say at a Committee meeting may be able to do so by way of a written submission or by applying to attend in person.

Have Your Say

Although citizens can vote for their elected politician to speak on their behalf, the voting process does not allow for detailed perusal of individual Bills or subjects that are presented to Parliament. Committees are a way that ordinary people can have a say in matters being discussed in Parliament.

Parliamentary Committees can be set up by the Senate, the House of Representatives, or by both together as a Joint Committee.

OFFICIAL ROLES IN PARLIAMENT

Here are some of the official roles that politicians and other people undertake to keep Parliament running smoothly...

THE SENATE + **THE HOUSE OF REPRESENTATIVES**

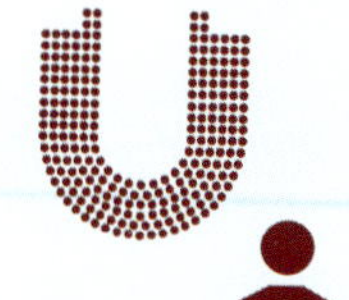

President – Head of the Australian Senate

Speaker – Head of the House of Representatives

Usher of the Black Rod – Officer in the Senate

Serjeant-at-arms – Officer in the House of Representatives

GOVERNMENT

Prime Minister – Leader of the party or group forming Government

Deputy Prime Minister

Leader of the Government in the Senate

Ministers – Members of Government who head a Department

Backbenchers – Members of the Government who are not ministers or special office holders

OPPOSITION

Opposition Leader – Leader of the party or group with the second highest number of people elected to the House of Representatives

Deputy Leader of the Opposition

Leader of the Opposition in the Senate

Shadow Ministers – Members of the Opposition who look after matters that would be those of a Department

Backbenchers – Members of the Opposition who are not shadow ministers or special office holders

The House of Representatives

PRESS GALLERY

The Press Gallery refers to the journalists who report on the happenings in Parliament. They have office facilities as well as special sections set aside for them to sit and watch the speeches.

Press Facilities

The seating for journalists is at one end of the House of Representatives and the Senate chambers. It is reserved for members of the media to take their notes and photographs. There are also offices in Parliament House where journalists can write their reports, or prepare their radio and television programs.

GLOSSARY

abruptly .... very suddenly

assent .... approval

bicameral .... having two houses of parliament

constituent .... voter in an electorate

democracy .... form of government elected by the people

electorate .... defined area in which a voter lives

Ministers .... MP or Senator responsible for a department

Monarch .... King or Queen

MP .... elected Member of Parliament in the Lower House

perusal .... examination of something

INDEX

Acknowledgements

Abbreviations: l–left, r–right, b–bottom, t–top, c–centre, m–middle

We would like to thank the following for permission to reproduce photographs (images © Shutterstock unless otherwise stated): p2tr FiledIMAGE/Shutterstock.com, p3ml Nils Versemann/Shutterstock.com, p3bl Nils VersemannShutterstock.com, p4tl State Library of New South Wales, Public domain, via Wikimedia Commons, p5ml FiledIMAGE/Shutterstock.com, p5mr ChameleonsEye/Shutterstock.com, p5br Tom Roberts. Public domain. via Wikimedia Commons, p6tr Australian Electoral Commission, CC BY 3.0 <https://creativecommons.org/licenses/by/3.0>, via Wikimedia Commons, p7ml UK Parliament, CC BY 3.0 <https://creativecommons.org/licenses/by/3.0>, via Wikimedia Commons, p7tr FiledIMAGE/Shutterstock.com, p7br Nils Versemann/Shutterstock.com, p8tl GillianVann/Shutterstock.com, p9tl UK government, OGL 3 <http://www.nationalarchives.gov.uk/doc/open-government-licence/version/3>, via Wikimedia Commons, p9br FiledIMAGE/Shutterstock.com, p9bl Nils Versemann/Shutterstock.com, p10tl Adam Schultz, Public domain, via Wikimedia Commons, p10mr attribute <gg.gov.au>, p12bc Nils Versemann/Shutterstock.com, p13bl Michael Tubi/Shutterstock.com, p14ml Tooykrub/Shutterstock.com, p15br CSIRO, CC BY 3.0 <https://creativecommons.org/licenses/by/3.0>, via Wikimedia Commons, p16-17c ChameleonsEye/Shutterstock.com, p16ml ukhouseoflords, CC BY 2.0 <https://creativecommons.org/licenses/by/2.0>, via Wikimedia Commons, p16mr Office of the Clerk/Parliamentary Service, CC BY 4.0 <https://creativecommons.org/licenses/by/4.0>, via Wikimedia Commons, p17tr Sergey Goryachev/Shutterstock.com, p18tl Office of the Clerk/Parliamentary Service, CC BY 4.0 <https://creativecommons.org/licenses/by/4.0>, via Wikimedia Commons, p19b Cpl. Angel Serna, Public domain, via Wikimedia Commons, p20tr Jimbo_Cymru/Shutterstock.com, p21tl Photographs by Gnangarra...commons.wikimedia.org, CC BY 2.5 AU <https://creativecommons.org/licenses/by/2.5/au/deed.en>, via Wikimedia Commons, p21tl Photographs by Gnangarra...commons.wikimedia.org, CC BY 2.5 AU <https://creativecommons.org/licenses/by/2.5/au/deed.en>, via Wikimedia Commons, p22br Kristin Greenwood/Shutterstock.com, p24-25c Greg Brave/Shutterstock.com, p27tr Hamiltonstone, CC BY-SA 3.0 <https://creativecommons.org/licenses/by-sa/3.0>, via Wikimedia Commons, p29b JJ Harrison (https://www.jjharrison.com.au/), CC BY-SA 3.0 <https://creativecommons.org/licenses/by-sa/3.0>, via Wikimedia Commons, p32tl ChameleonsEye/Shutterstock.com, p32bl Nils Versemann/Shutterstock.com, p32br JJ Harrison (https://www.jjharrison.com.au/), CC BY-SA 3.0 <https://creativecommons.org/licenses/by-sa/3.0>, via Wikimedia Commons

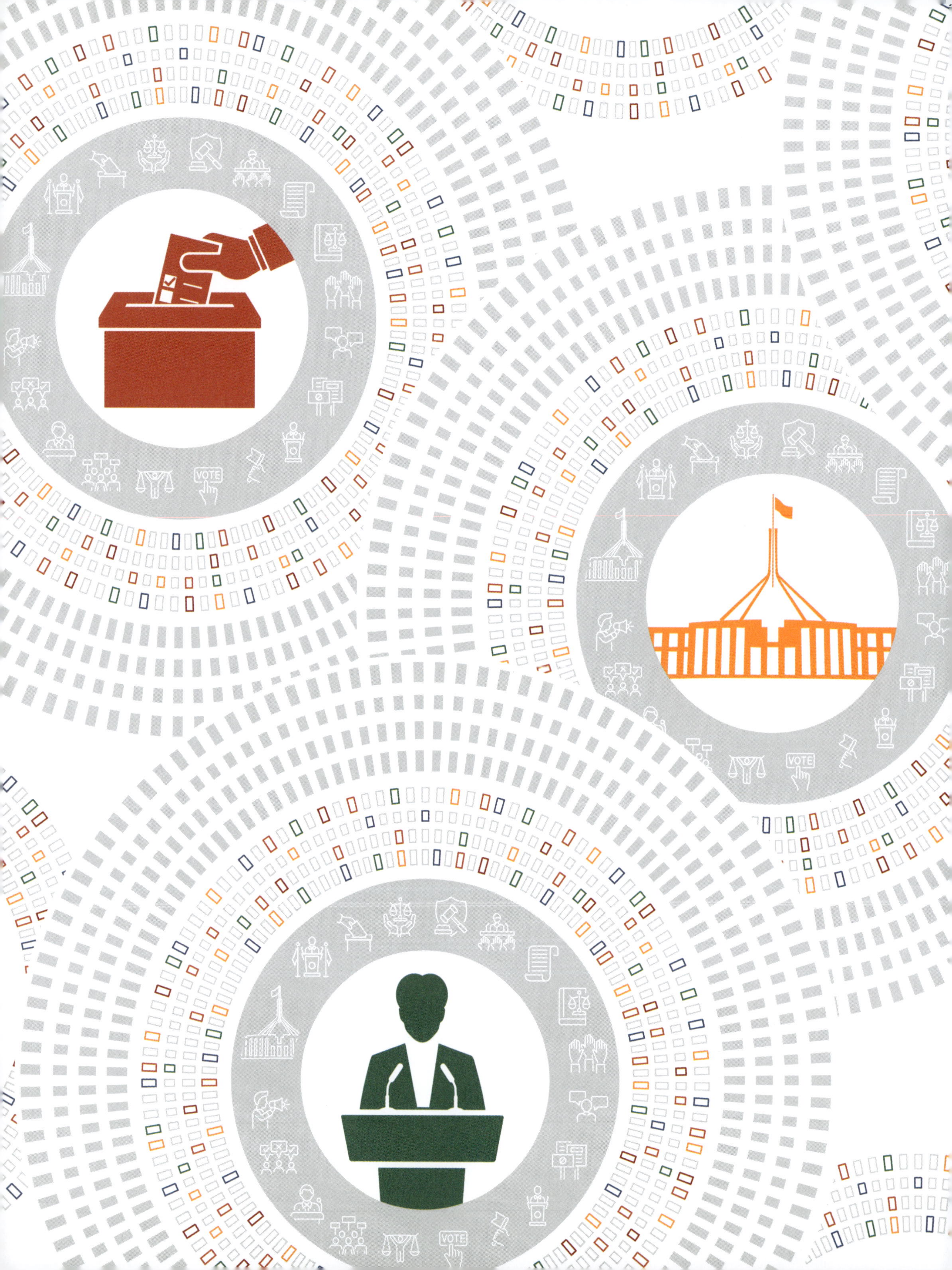
VOTE
VOTE
VOTE